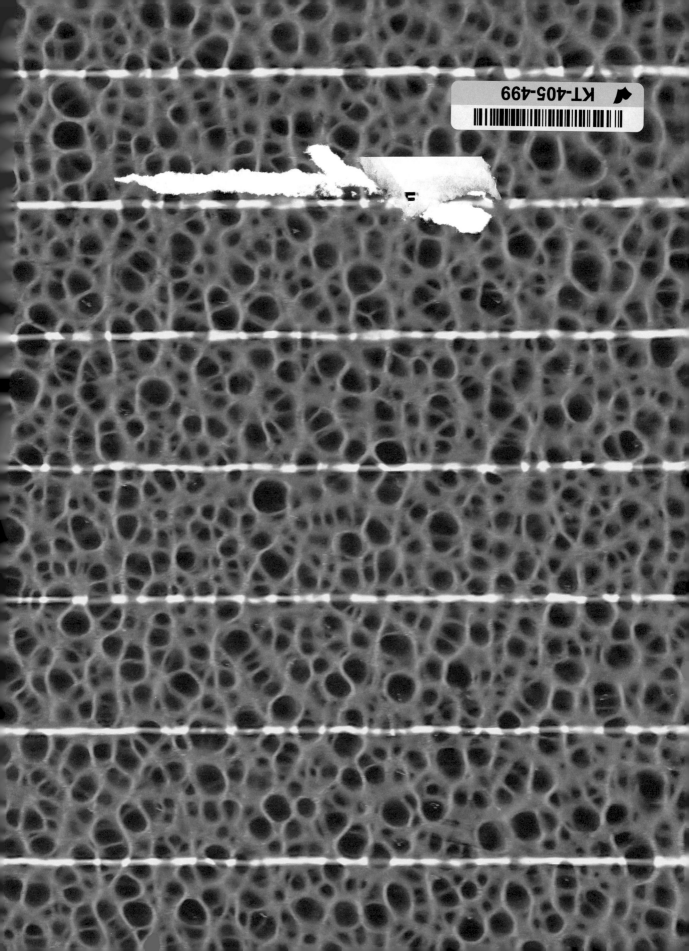

SCIENCE
IS EVERYWHERE

FUELLING UP

Energy, global warming and renewables

Rob Colson

WAYLAND

First published in Great Britain
in 2017 by Wayland
Copyright © Hodder and Stoughton, 2017

Wayland
An imprint of Hachette
Children's Group
Part of Hodder and Stoughton
Carmelite House
50 Victoria Embankment
London EC4Y 0DZ

Executive editor: Adrian Cole
Produced by Tall Tree Ltd
Written by: Rob Colson
Designer: Ben Ruocco

ISBN: 978 1 5263 0502 2
10 9 8 7 6 5 4 3 2 1

An Hachette UK Company
www.hachette.co.uk
www.hachettechildrens.co.uk

Printed and bound in China

The website addresses (URLs) included
in this book were valid at the time of
going to press. However, it is possible
that contents or addresses may have
changed since the publication of this book.
No responsibility for any such changes
can be accepted by either the author or
the Publisher.

MIX
Paper from
responsible sources
FSC
www.fsc.org
FSC® C104740

t-top, b-bottom, l-left, r-right, c-centre,
front cover-fc, back cover-bc
All images courtesy of Dreamstime.com,
unless indicated:
Inside front Victority; fc, bc Pablo631;
fctr Darrenbaker; fcbr Byronwmoore;
fcbl Meryll; bctr Mailthepic; bctl, 19cl
Ieva; bccl Sakuragirin; 1cl, 24-25
Choneschones; 1cl, 24l Bestvc; 4t Epixx;
5tr Lucadp; 4-5b Yauhen Paleski; 6t
Ironrodart; 6bl Vladimir Yudin; 7t,
27r Aona2303; 7tc Arm2528; 8t, 27tr
Alhovik; 9br Mishkacz; 11t Alvinsevsk29;
11b Gelpi; 11br Andrei Krauchuk; 12-13t
NASA; 12-13t Dutchscenery; 14b Artjazz;
15t, 18b, Andreadonetti; 15tl Prillfoto;
16lc Photka; 16cr Pattarawit Chompipat;
16bl Akel150sb; 17tl Editor77; 17br
Rob1713; 18cl Paulmichaelhughes; 19cr
Kostiuchenko; 19bc Katya Triling; 21tl
Bedo; 21cr Lindenblade; 21b Dinozzaver;
22tr, 31tr Yudesign; 22bl Hyrons; 23br
Chagpg; 24tr Olivier Le Queinec; 25t
Photomall; 26-27t Henriklundgren;
27cr Vedexent/CC BY 4.0 http://
creativecommons.org/licenses/by/4.0/;
28b Maxxyustas; 28tr Discovod; 29tr
Mexrix; 29tr Anweber; 29cr Jesseterr;
29b Pavlo Syvak; 30tl Sirikul; 30cr
Igor Netkov; 30b Tomplesnik; 32t
Stylephotographs

Every attempt has been made to
clear copyright. Should there be any
inadvertent omission please apply to the
publisher for rectification.

Contents

What is energy?

Energy is the ability to do work – to change or move something in the world. Energy cannot be created or destroyed, only changed from one form to another. Fuel is a source of energy that we change into forms, such as electricity, that allow us to do work.

Ping pong ball

Kinetic energy

Kinetic energy is the energy an object has because it is **moving**. It is **equal** to the amount of energy it would take to stop the object from moving.

The heavier golf ball has more kinetic energy, so it will make a bigger **splash**.

Potential energy

Potential energy is energy stored in an object because of where it is. On Earth, an object has potential energy if it is lifted **off the ground**. Lifting works against **Earth's gravity**, and the object's potential energy will be converted into kinetic energy if it is **allowed to drop**.

The cyclist pedals hard up the hill, converting this work into **potential energy**.

Chemical energy

Golf ball

Chemical energy is the energy stored in the bonds between atoms and molecules in a substance. It can be released by a chemical reaction, often turning the energy into the form of heat. Batteries store energy in the form of chemical energy.

Impossible machines

For centuries, inventors have tried to design a machine that runs forever **without fuel**, known as a **perpetual motion** machine. However, all machines will eventually stop due to friction and other forces, unless they have energy put into them. The Italian inventor **Leonardo da Vinci** (1452–1519) attempted to design a wheel that would turn forever with the help of moving balls. In reality, friction would make the wheel stop very quickly.

"Wheeee eeeeeee!"

Riding down the hill, the cyclist can **freewheel**, as the potential energy is changed into kinetic energy.

Fossil fuels

Fossil fuels are a form of chemical energy stored in the ground. They are the remains of dead plants and animals that have been buried and compressed over millions of years. We can turn this energy into heat by burning fossil fuels.

Coal

Coal is a solid fossil fuel that is **mined from the ground**. It is made from the remains of ancient trees that have been **compressed** to form a hard black rock.

Coal forms layers of rock called seams. Coal seams range from just a few millimetres to more than 15 metres in thickness.

Oil and gas

Oil and gas are found deep underground, and are extracted by **drilling deep into rocks**. They formed from the remains of marine animals and plants, which fell to the **bottom of the ocean** and were **trapped under mud**. The remains were **buried and squashed** to form oil and gas that were trapped under the rocks.

Rock

Gas

Oil

Captured energy

The energy in fossil fuels came originally from **the Sun**. The Sun's energy was **captured by plants**, which turned it into chemical energy. This energy is **released as heat** when the fossil fuels are burned.

Generating electricity

Fossil fuels can be used to produce **electricity**. The **heat** from burning fuel is used to heat water, producing **steam**. The moving steam then turns huge **turbines**. The **kinetic energy** in the turbines is transformed into electricity.

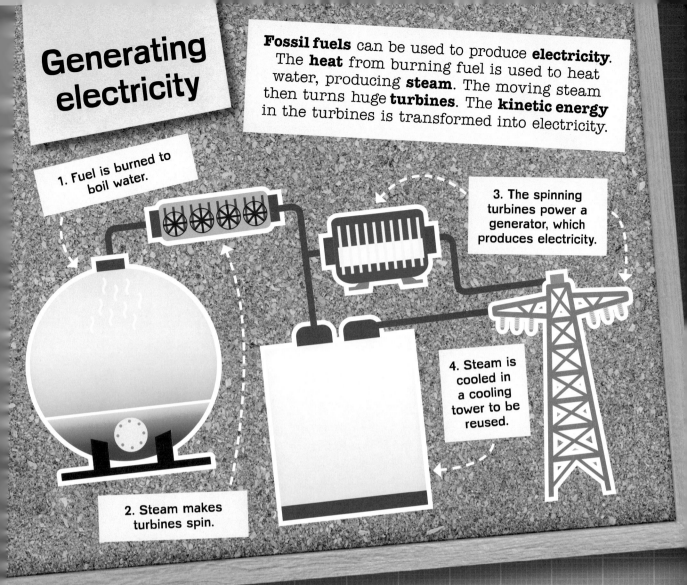

1. Fuel is burned to boil water.

3. The spinning turbines power a generator, which produces electricity.

4. Steam is cooled in a cooling tower to be reused.

2. Steam makes turbines spin.

TRY THIS

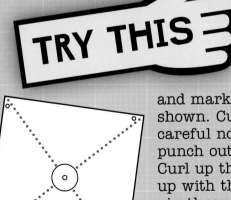

Make a pinwheel turbine
You will need: paper, a drawing pin, a ruler and a pencil with a rubber on the end.

Cut out a square of paper and mark it with a pencil and ruler as shown. Cut along the dotted lines, being careful not to cut right to the centre, and punch out the holes with a drawing pin. Curl up the corner holes so that they line up with the centre hole. Push the drawing pin through all the holes and into the side of the pencil rubber. Hold the pencil and blow into the pinwheel to make it spin.

Global warming

When fossil fuels are burned, they release the gas carbon dioxide (CO_2) into the atmosphere. This is causing our planet to heat up.

The greenhouse effect

Adding **carbon dioxide to the atmosphere** speeds up a process called the greenhouse effect. About half of the rays from the Sun are reflected back into space. The other half heat the surface of Earth, which gives off heat as infrared radiation. Some of this radiation escapes into space, but the rest is reflected back to Earth by carbon dioxide and other gases, known as **greenhouse gases**, in the atmosphere.

The **average temperature** at Earth's surface is about 15°Celsius (C). Greenhouse gases occur naturally in the atmosphere, and without them, the planet would be **more than 10°C colder than it is**. However, the level of carbon dioxide in the atmosphere has risen by **one third in the last 200 years** due to industrial activity by humans.

Half of Sun's rays reflected into space

Half of Sun's rays warm Earth

Tackling climate change

In the future, we will need to produce energy without releasing

CO_2 into the atmosphere.

Some people support the use of more nuclear power. However, this also creates **dangerous waste**, and nuclear power stations are at risk of serious accidents. We also need to move over to clean energy sources, such as **solar power**, and to **use energy more efficiently.**

If we do not cut our carbon dioxide emissions, scientists predict that the average temperature could **rise by up to 5°C** during the 21st century. This would result in **melting of the ice** at the poles and **rising sea levels**. Low-lying countries such as Bangladesh would face widespread flooding. In 1997, most of the world's governments signed up to the

Kyoto Protocol,

in which they committed to cutting carbon dioxide emissions in order to limit global warming to less than 2°C.

Earth gives off heat

Greenhouse gases reflect some heat back to Earth

TRY THIS

What you need to see the greenhouse effect in action:

Two thermometers and a sealable glass jar large enough to fit one of the thermometers.

First place both thermometers in direct sunlight for three minutes. Record the temperature, then seal one of the thermometers in the jar and place them both back in the sunlight for another ten minutes. Now record the temperatures shown by the thermometers once more.

How much has the temperature risen inside the jar? Why do you think this is?

Going nuclear

The heat needed to drive the turbines of a power station can be created using nuclear energy. Nuclear power plants release energy that is stored in the nuclei of atoms. The physicist Albert Einstein (1879–1955) was the first person to show that matter can be turned into energy. Einstein's famous equation $E = mc^2$ describes how a small amount of mass (m) can be changed into a large amount of energy (E).

Splitting the atom

The nuclear reactions that produce energy take place on a microscopic scale, within the atoms of the **chemical element uranium**. More than a million uranium atoms could sit on a pinhead. The nucleus at the centre of the uranium atoms is split when it is hit by an even smaller particle called a **neutron**. The reaction produces more neutrons, which hit other nuclei, triggering a

chain reaction

in which a huge number of atoms are split very quickly. Each reaction turns some of the mass of the uranium into heat.

Neutron hits uranium nucleus

Uranium nucleus splits into smaller nuclei and more neutrons

Neutrons hit more uranium nuclei

Dangerous waste

Nuclear reactors produce radioactive waste. This material can remain harmful for thousands of years and needs to be safely stored encased in glass deep underground.

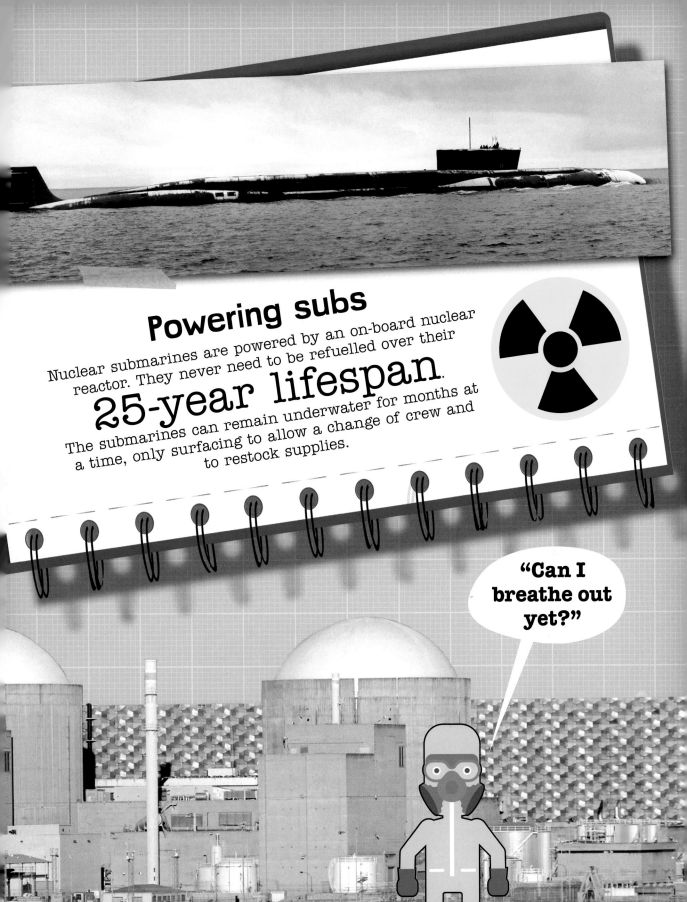

Powering subs

Nuclear submarines are powered by an on-board nuclear reactor. They never need to be refuelled over their 25-year lifespan. The submarines can remain underwater for months at a time, only surfacing to allow a change of crew and to restock supplies.

"Can I breathe out yet?"

Energy from the Sun

Sunlight is a clean source of energy that will never run out, known as a renewable energy. Several technologies have been developed to capture this energy.

Light into electricity

Photovoltaic cells turn the energy in sunlight directly into electricity. The cost of producing solar panels covered in photovoltaic cells has fallen dramatically and today about

1 per cent of the world's energy
is produced using them.

Millions of homes in Germany now have solar panels on their roofs. **Six per cent** of Germany's electricity is generated by solar panels such as these.

Concentrated heat

TRY THIS

Parabolic reflectors work by focusing the heat from the Sun onto **a tube** containing **liquid oil**. The oil is heated to temperatures of

up to 400°C,

and used to produce steam to power a turbine.

Absorber tube

Focal point

Reflector

The trough is the shape of a parabola, and reflects sunlight towards a focal point along which the pipe of oil runs.

The warmth of the Sun produces currents of air called updraughts. Harness the power of an updraught with a solar updraught tower.

Tape together end-to-end three cleaned empty cans with their tops and bottoms removed (ask an adult for help and beware sharp edges). Unbend a paper clip to create an arch. Tape the arch to the top of the tower. Tape a drawing pin to the top of the arch with the point up, and stick a pinwheel (see page 7) to the pin. Now balance your tower on two books with a gap between them to allow the air in, and place in sunlight. An updraught will make the pinwheel spin.

Renewables
around the world

In addition to solar power, many other sources of renewable energy can be used to generate electricity. Different parts of the world are particularly suited to different forms of renewables.

Wind power

Wind turbines turn the power of the wind into electricity.

Wind turbines are often placed at sea to take advantage of windy offshore conditions, such as those found in the North Sea.

Water power

Hydroelectric power stations **power turbines using moving water**. The largest power station in the world is a hydroelectric power station in China called the

Three Gorges Dam.

Such huge dams generate **clean energy**, but they also flood large areas of land. More than a million people had to move home when the Three Gorges Dam was built.

Twice a day, the oceans rise and fall due to the gravitational pull of the Moon and the Sun. These tidal changes can be harnessed to power turbines both as the tide comes in and as it goes out. Areas with large differences between the levels of high and low tide are suitable for tidal power plants. The world's first tidal power station was built across the estuary of the River Rance in northern France in 1966.

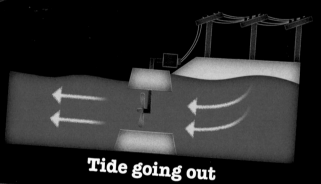

Tide coming in

Tide going out

Geothermal power

Underneath Earth's rocky crust is

hot magma

at a temperature of more than 1000°C. The rock near this magma deep underground can be very hot. Geothermal power stations produce steam for turbines **by heating water in this hot underground rock**. Geothermal power stations are very effective in places such as Iceland and New Zealand that are located at boundaries between the tectonic plates that make up Earth's crust.

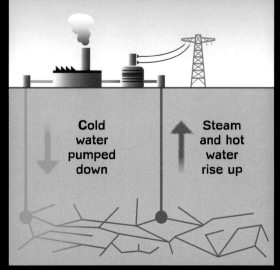

Cold water pumped down

Steam and hot water rise up

Filling up

Most cars run on fuel made from crude oil, such as petrol or diesel. The fuel burns inside the engine to provide power.

Piston power

An engine's pistons move up and down inside cylinders in a four-stroke cycle. In the intake stroke (1), the piston moves down, sucking in fuel and air. In the compression stroke (2), the piston moves up, squeezing the fuel and air. The fuel is set alight by a spark plug, pushing the piston down in the power stroke (3). The piston moves up and waste gases are pushed out in the exhaust stroke (4).

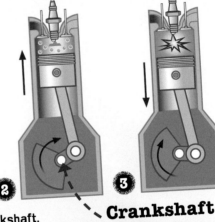

Crankshaft

Pumping pistons power the engine's crankshaft.

Exhaust fumes

The waste from burning the fuel is removed from the car through the exhaust pipes. Exhaust fumes include harmful gases such as **carbon monoxide**. Cars that run on diesel fuel also give off fine particles of soot, which are particularly damaging to the

health of people.

Electric cars

Electric cars are driven by an **electric motor**. They do not produce exhaust fumes, but their batteries need to be **recharged** regularly by plugging the cars into the mains.

Hybrids

A hybrid vehicle is driven by both a **petrol engine** and an **electric motor**. Energy produced when the vehicle brakes is used to charge batteries that **power the motor**.

This makes the vehicle more efficient and cleaner than those with just a petrol engine. The fumes from road vehicles cause damaging smog in large cities. Many cities are now encouraging electric cars and switching their buses over to cleaner hybrid technology. The car manufacturer Ford now plans to produce a hybrid car that has **solar panels** on its roof.

Many new school buses in the US are hybrid vehicles.

SCHOOL BUS

226

17

An electric world

If you look around you, most of the machines you use today are powered by electricity.

Electric circuit

Electricity is caused by the movement of tiny particles called electrons. Electrons have a negative charge. Negatively charged particles are attracted to positively charged particles, so electrons flow towards an area with positive charge. Electrons can only flow if there is a complete circuit from an area of positive charge to an area of negative charge. A material called a conductor is needed to allow the electricity to flow.

Resistor

The resistor, such as a light bulb, takes energy from the electric circuit, turning it into other forms of energy such as light or heat.

Conductor

Battery

Switch

How a battery works

A battery converts **chemical energy** into **electricity**. A battery has a positively charged end **(the cathode)** and a negatively charged end **(the anode)**, separated by a fluid called an **electrolyte**. A chemical reaction inside the battery creates an excess of electrons at the anode. When the anode and cathode are connected, electrons flow from the anode to the cathode. A battery becomes flat when the excess of electrons at the anode has been exhausted. Recharging a battery uses electricity to reverse the process.

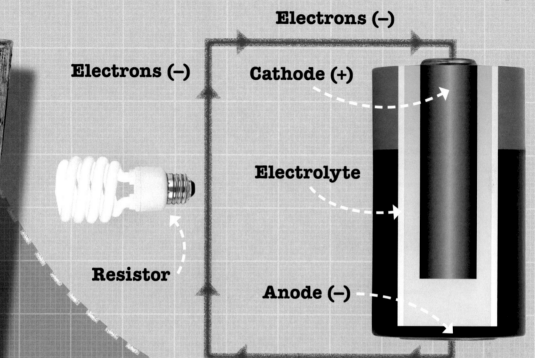

Electrons (–)

Electrons (–)

Cathode (+)

Electrolyte

Resistor

Anode (–)

Electrons (–)

TRY THIS

The chemical energy stored in a potato can be used to make a battery.

What you need:
A large fresh potato, two leads with alligator clips at either end, a small LED, a galvanised (zinc-covered) nail and a copper coin.

Insert the nail and the coin into the potato a couple of centimetres apart. Connect one lead to the nail and the other to the coin, and connect the other ends of the leads to opposite sides of the LED. This completes an electric circuit. Does your LED glow?

Growing your fuel

An alternative to fossil fuels is fuel produced by living things. This fuel is called biofuel and takes many different forms.

Gasohol

Alcohol made from **sugar cane** can be mixed with petrol to help power car engines. Known as **gasohol**, this **biofuel** is widely used in Brazil.

Biogas

Biogas is a mixture of the gases **methane and carbon dioxide** that are produced by **food and dung** when they rot in an atmosphere **without oxygen**. The methane can be burned to produce electricity or to heat water. It is an important fuel in places that are not linked up to an electricity grid, and provides a useful way to **recycle cow manure** on farms.

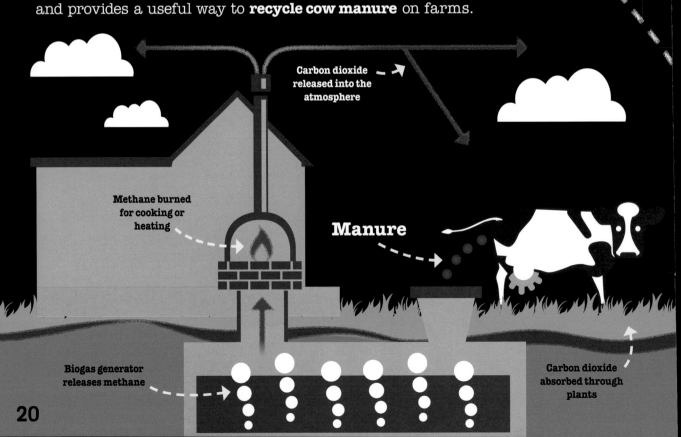

Carbon dioxide released into the atmosphere

Methane burned for cooking or heating

Manure

Biogas generator releases methane

Carbon dioxide absorbed through plants

Algae-power

Many people criticise biofuels such as gasohol because they take land and **fresh water** that could be used to grow crops **for food**. Fuel can also be made from the

oil in algae,

which grow in salt water. Airliners around the world are conducting trials with algae fuel to power the jet engines of their aircraft.

This algae farm field in Indonesia could one day make the fuel that powers aircraft.

Magnetic power

Magnetism is a property closely related to electricity. Wherever there is an electric current, there will be a magnetic field surrounding it. Magnets produce forces that attract magnetic materials such as iron.

A magnet has two poles: North and South. Opposite poles attract, while similar poles repel one another.

N **S**

Electromagnets

Any electric current produces a magnetic field around it. Electromagnets are magnets produced by **passing electricity through a conductor**. They can be powerful enough to lift a car.

Electromagnetic induction

In 1831, the English scientist **Michael Faraday** (1791–1867) discovered electromagnetic induction. He showed that a moving magnetic field can induce (create) an electric current in any material that **conducts electricity**. This is the principle behind electricity generators and electric motors.

Generators

In a power station, the generator converts the kinetic energy of a **spinning turbine** into electricity using **electromagnetic induction**. The turbine spins a magnet inside a **copper stator**. The moving magnetic field induces an electric **current** in the copper.

Spinning magnet

Copper stator

Electric current

Turbine

TRY THIS

Electric motor

Electric motors work in the **reverse way** to generators, turning an electric current into **spinning motion**. Motors are found inside all kinds of machines, from washing machines to computers.

Make a magnetic needle

What you need:
A bar magnet and a needle.

Use one end of the magnet to stroke the needle in the same direction 50 times from end to end. Now see which materials you can pick up with the needle. Can it pick up paper clips? Try stroking another needle 100 times.
Is this magnet stronger?

Magnetic tracks

The fastest trains in the world are powered by magnetism.

Maglev trains

hover a few centimetres above a magnetic field. A powerful electromagnet pushes the trains along the track at speeds of up to 603 km/h.

Saving energy

More than half the electricity consumption of a typical home is used for heating and cooling, while about 20 per cent is used for lighting. Saving energy at home reduces the need to generate electricity, saving money and helping the environment.

Homes were first linked up to electricity in the late 19th century. The first electrified homes were lit using

incandescent

light bulbs, which pass electricity through a thin **metal filament**. The filament glowed brightly, but about **95 per cent** of the energy was given off as heat rather than light. In recent years, incandescent lighting has been replaced by more efficient systems.

Fluorescent

lights produce light by passing

electricity through a gas.

They are much more efficient than incandescent light bulbs, but they take some time to reach **full brightness**. They also contain poisonous mercury, which means that they need to be disposed of very carefully.

Light-emitting diodes (LEDs)

pass electricity through materials called **semi-conductors**, which give off light of a single colour when the current is at a certain strength. LEDs produce

very little heat

and are even more energy-efficient than fluorescent lights and **safer to dispose of**. They also reach full brightness almost instantly, like incandescent bulbs. A white light can be made by mixing diodes of

different colours.

Green homes

The passive house is a home that uses less than

20 per cent

of the energy for heating and cooling ordinary homes. During winter, **warm stale air** from inside the house is used to heat **fresh, colder air** entering the house through the **heat recovery and ventilation system (MVHR)**. During summer, **the reverse** happens. This greatly reduces the amount of energy needed to maintain the **right temperature** inside the house.

Cold fresh air in

MVHR

Cold stale air out

Airtight building

Warm stale air out

Warm fresh air in

Insulation

Triple-glazed windows

Energy of the future

The amount of energy reaching Earth from the Sun in one hour would be enough to power the whole world for a year. Scientists are looking for radical new ways to capture more of this energy. It may even be possible to make energy on Earth the same way the Sun makes its energy.

Solar panels in space

Scientists in Japan are working on a project to put solar panels into space. Unlike panels on Earth, these panels would face the Sun **24 hours a day** and would not be affected by Earth's atmosphere, meaning that they would produce **10 times as much energy**. Each panel would be a square measuring 2 kilometres across. They would send the energy down to Earth as a **beam of microwave energy**, which would be captured by a floating receiver.

Microwave beam

Floating receiver

Heat from
the Sun

Solar
panels
in space

Nuclear
fusion

The Sun produces its
energy through a process
called **nuclear fusion**, in
which hydrogen atoms fuse
together to form helium
atoms, releasing energy in
the process. Nuclear fusion
could potentially be a

clean form

of energy, but the process
requires heating gas to millions
of degrees Celsius. Scientists have
not yet overcome the problem of
how to keep such a super-hot gas
confined in one place.

Dyson
sphere

In 1937, the British science fiction writer
Olaf Stapledon (1886–1950) proposed
the idea of surrounding the Sun with a
sphere that would collect its energy and
beam it back to us. It has been named the
Dyson sphere after a mathematician who
developed the idea. Astronomers searching
for alien life have suggested looking for
evidence of Dyson spheres, as they think
advanced civilisations may have built one
around their nearest star.

Can
you
help?

The website
climateprediction.net is
running a climate-modelling
project that links up
computers across the
world to produce more
accurate predictions about
global warming. Anybody
with a home computer
can sign up to help.

27

Quiz

1 Which kind of **power station** produces

radioactive waste?

a) Nuclear power stations
b) Oil-fired power stations
c) Geothermal power stations

2 ## Batteries

store energy in which form?
a) Potential energy
b) Chemical energy
c) Kinetic energy

3 What is the collective name for fuels such as **coal, oil and natural gas** that are formed from the remains of dead organisms?

4 Coal-fired power stations turn the **chemical energy** stored in coal into

electricity.

Describe the changes the energy goes through from **the start to the end of this process**, including the names of the kind of energy produced at each stage.

"How did you get up there?"

5 **Global warming** is caused by an increase in levels **of which gas** in the atmosphere?
a) Carbon dioxide
b) Carbon monoxide
c) Water vapour

6 **Photovoltaic cells** produce electricity using which source of

energy?

a) Wind
b) Geothermal
c) Sunlight

7 In a charged battery, an excess of electrons gathers at which end, **the cathode** or **the anode**?

8 Name three examples of **renewable** energy sources.

9 Name the **two power sources** that drive a hybrid vehicle.

12 A generator turns the **spinning motion** of a **magnet** into electricity using which scientific principle?

13 An **incandescent light bulb** gives off **95 per cent** of its energy in which form?
a) Light
b) Heat
c) Spinning motion

10 **Gasohol** is a fuel made by mixing petrol with alcohol made from **which plant?**

11 Electricity along power lines is produced by **the flow** of which charged **particles?**

14 Name two reasons why solar panels are **more efficient** in space than on the surface of Earth.

Glossary

Biofuel
A fuel made from living matter.

Chemical energy
A form of energy stored in the bonds of atoms and molecules.

Electricity
A form of energy that results from the movement of negatively charged electrons along a conductor.

Electromagnetic induction
The process by which an electrical current is produced in a conductor by the presence of a moving magnetic field.

Fossil fuel
A store of energy found in the ground, such as coal or oil, that is made from the remains of living organisms.

Geothermal energy
Heat energy found in Earth's crust. Where this heat energy rises near the surface of the crust it can be used to generate electricity.

Greenhouse effect
The warming of Earth caused by the presence of gases such as carbon dioxide in the atmosphere. The gases reflect some of the heat given off by Earth's surface back down to Earth, preventing it from escaping into space.

Hybrid
A vehicle that is powered by both a petrol engine and an electric motor.

Hydroelectric power
A way of generating electricity using moving water.

Kinetic energy
A form of energy that an object has due to its movement.

Light-emitting diode (LED)
A device that gives off light when an electric current is passed through it. Light bulbs that use LEDs are very efficient as little of the energy is lost as heat.

Nuclear reaction
A process by which the nucleus of an atom is changed by being split apart or joined with the nucleus of another atom. Nuclear power stations use the energy released by nuclear reactions to generate electricity.

Photovoltaic cell
A device that converts light into an electric current. Solar panels are made from photovoltaic cells.

Potential energy
A form of energy that an object has due to its position relative to other objects.

Turbine
A machine with blades that are turned by a flow of liquid or gas. Spinning turbines are used in power stations to generate electricity.

Index

Answers

1. a) Nuclear power stations
2. b) Chemical energy
3. Fossil fuels
4. The chemical energy in the coal is turned into heat energy by burning it. The heat energy is turned into kinetic energy by passing steam through turbines. The kinetic energy in the turbines is turned into electricity by the generator.
5. a) Carbon dioxide
6. c) Sunlight
7. The anode
8. You could have said solar, wind, hydroelectric, tidal or geothermal
9. A petrol engine and an electric motor
10. Sugar cane
11. Electrons
12. Electromagnetic induction
13. b) Heat
14. They can face the Sun 24 hours a day, and the intensity of the sunlight is not reduced by passing through Earth's atmosphere.

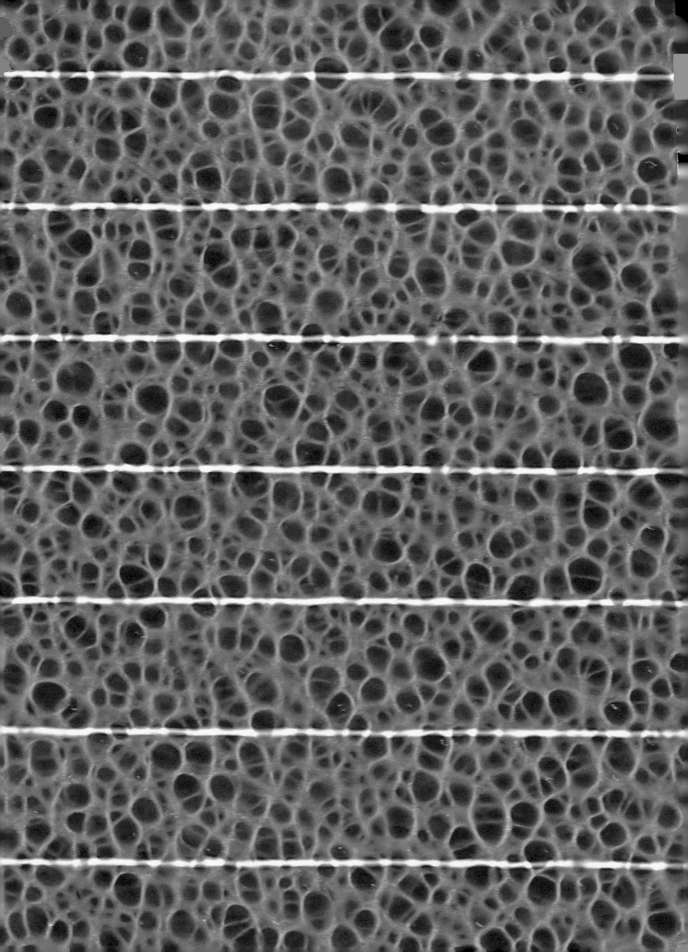